Gideon looked around.
Gideon didn't want anyone to see him.

He didn't want to get caught.

If the enemy soldiers saw Gideon, they
would steal his grain.
Gideon needed grain to make bread.
His family needed to eat.

Gideon hit the grain with his stick.
He hit the grain again and again.
The good grain came off the stalk.

Gideon was careful.
He worked quietly.
He worked quickly.
He didn't want to get caught.

Gideon sneaked back to hide
in his cave.
His whole family was hiding in
the cave.
They were hiding from the
enemy soldiers.

The enemy soldiers had taken
Gideon's house.
They had taken Gideon's farm.
They had taken the donkeys and cows.
They had taken all the food.
Now Gideon's family had to hide.

Gideon's friends had lost their houses.
Gideon's friends had lost their
farms too.
They were hiding in caves.
They were hiding in the hills too.

Every day Gideon beat more grain
with his stick.
He was careful.
He worked quietly.
He worked quickly.
He didn't want to get caught.

One day, God talked to Gideon.
God said, "Gideon, I want you to lead
My army.
I will help you fight the enemy
soldiers.
You will win."

God said, "Call your friends from
the caves.
Call your friends from the hills.
Your friends will be a mighty army.
Your friends will be the Lord's army."

Gideon called to his friends.
Gideon talked to many men.
They came together.
They made a big army.

The Lord's army was very big.
God said, "There are too many people.
We don't need so many.
The Lord's army should not be so big.
Tell the people, 'If you are afraid, you
can go home.'"

Many people went home.

God said, "There are still too many people.
We don't need so many.
The Lord's army should not be so big."

More people went home.
Many more people went home.
The Lord's army was very small.

But God said to Gideon, "This is
the Lord's army.
You will win.
You will win with this army.
Tonight you may sneak down to
the enemy.
Tonight you may listen to the
enemy soldiers."

Gideon and his friend looked down at
the enemy soldiers' tents.
There were tents everywhere.
There were soldiers everywhere.
The enemy army was very big.
The enemy army was gigantic!

When it was dark, Gideon and his
friend snuck down the hill.
They were careful.
They crawled quietly.
They crawled quickly.
They didn't want to get caught.

Gideon and his friend crawled up to a tent.
They listened quietly.
One of the enemy soldiers said, "Gideon will win.
Gideon will win the battle."

Gideon was happy.
Gideon knew God would help him.
He knew the Lord's army would win.
He and his friend snuck back
to their camp.

Gideon went back to his camp.
He called his men together.

He gave everyone a torch to hide
in a jar.
He gave everyone a trumpet.

Gideon said, "Do what I do.
God is with us."

Gideon and the Lord's army waited in the dark.

They snuck down the hill.
They were careful.
They crawled quietly.
They crawled quickly.
They didn't want to get caught.

Gideon and the Lord's army made
a circle around the enemy soldiers.
Gideon and his men waited
until midnight.
It was very dark.
It was very quiet.

Gideon stood up tall.
He blew his trumpet.
Everyone in the Lord's army blew
their trumpets.

Gideon smashed his jar and held
his torch high.
The light shone brightly.

All the men in the Lord's army
smashed their jars.
Their torches shone brightly.

The Lord's army held up their torches.
The Lord's army blew their trumpets.
The Lord's army shouted, "A sword for the Lord!
A sword for Gideon!"

Gideon and the Lord's army
stood still.
They stood in the dark.
They stood in a circle.

The enemy soldiers woke up.

The enemy soldiers ran
around yelling.
The enemy soldiers got mixed up.
The enemy soldiers fought each other!

"A sword for the Lord," Gideon's men called.

"A sword for Gideon.
Hurray for the Lord's army!"

About the Author
Mary Manz Simon holds a doctoral degree in education with a specialty in early childhood education. She has taught at levels from preschool through postgraduate. Dr. Simon is the best-selling author of more than 40 children's books, including *Little Visits with Jesus*. She and her husband, the Reverend Henry A. Simon, are the parents of three children.